WEST COAST ADVENTURES

AMAZING STORIES

WEST COAST ADVENTURES

Shipwrecks, Lighthouses, and Rescues
Along Canada's West Coast

HISTORY/ADVENTURE
by Adrienne Mason

PUBLISHED BY ALTITUDE PUBLISHING CANADA LTD.
1500 Railway Avenue, Canmore, Alberta T1W 1P6
www.altitudepublishing.com
1-800-957-6888

Extreme care has been taken to ensure that all information presented in
this book is accurate and up to date. Neither the author nor the
publisher can be held responsible for any errors.

Publisher	Stephen Hutchings
Associate Publisher	Kara Turner
Editor	Lori Burwash

We acknowledge the financial support of the Government
of Canada through the Book Publishing Industry Development
Program (BPIDP) for our publishing activities.

Altitude GreenTree Program
Altitude Publishing will plant twice as many trees as were used
in the manufacturing of this product.

National Library of Canada Cataloguing in Publication Data
Mason, Adrienne
West Coast adventures / Adrienne Mason

(Amazing stories)
Includes bibliographical references.
ISBN 1-55153-990-X

1. Shipwrecks--British Columbia--Pacific Coast. 2. Pacific Coast (B.C.)--
History. I. Title. II. Series: Amazing stories (Canmore, Alta.)
FC3820.S5M38 2003   910.4'52   C2003-910168-1
G525.M38 2003

An application for the trademark for Amazing Stories™
has been made and the registered trademark is pending.

Printed and bound in Canada by Friesens
2 4 6 8 9 7 5 3

For John Boom and Ovid Eng

Contents

Map 10

Prologue 13

Chapter 1 The Rescue of the *Puritan* 15

Chapter 2 Honeymoon on the High Seas . 21

Chapter 3 Life on the Lights 37

Chapter 4 Coastal Lifeline 54

Chapter 5 Putting Bamfield on the Map . . 64

Chapter 6 The *Valencia* Tragedy 76

Chapter 7 Rescue of the *Coloma* 97

Bibliography 104

Graveyard of the Pacific

The southwest coast of Vancouver Island is often referred to as the "Graveyard of the Pacific" because of the concentration of wrecks there. Storms and the west coast's rugged coastline still claim lives and ships today.

PORT HARDY

PACIFIC

OCEAN

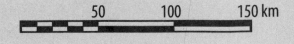

50   100   150 km

130°00'   128°00'

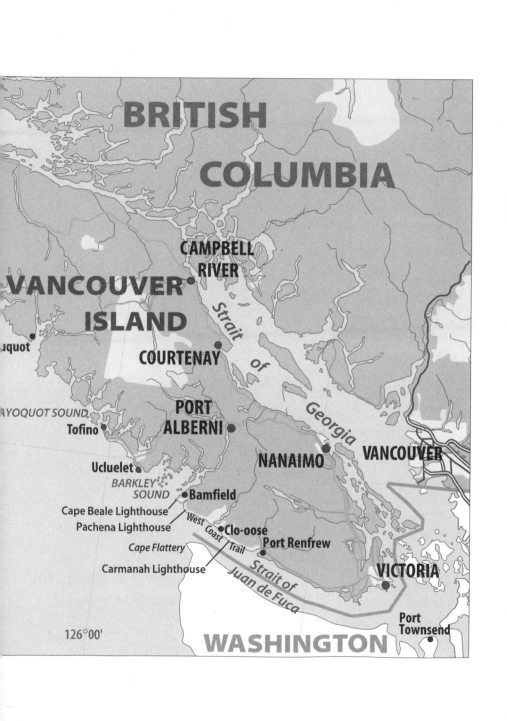

Prologue

It was a harrowing scene. Barefoot women and children clothed only in nightdresses were lashed to the ship's masts or clutched desperately to freezing rigging. Other passengers huddled on the deck under tarpaulins or blankets. The sea's onslaught was relentless — the ship shuddered and groaned with each wave. Sea foam and sleet swirled around them. Land was torturously close, only 30 or so metres away, but the sea and jagged reefs between the ruined ship and the sheer cliff must have seemed like a deliverance from one type of hell to another to those clinging to life on board.

While they awaited their fate — rescue or death — the survivors of the wreck endured mental torture, reliving the last several hours, when they had watched fully laden lifeboats flood and tip and unrelenting waves wash the decks clear of people. Now, as daylight lifted the veil on their surroundings, they could see the devastation — shattered bodies and ship's wreckage cast on shore or surging around them in the frothing sea. On this icy January morning, almost every survivor would have lost someone: husband, wife, mother, father, child, friend, perhaps a stranger they were only just beginning to know.

This was the scene of the final hours of the passenger ship Valencia, *which went ashore near Pachena Point, on the southwest coast of Vancouver Island, in January 1906. The wreck of the* Valencia, *in which at least 117 people died, is the BC coast's* Titanic.

Chapter 1
The Rescue of
the *Puritan*

N ovember 13, 1896. The crew of the Puritan stood on the deck of the four-masted schooner and looked desperately into the inky night, willing their eyes to see something, anything, through the fog and raging gale. The flash of a lighthouse beacon or a navigational buoy would at least give them some clue as to their whereabouts.

By Captain Atwood's calculations, they should have been nearing Tatoosh lighthouse and the entrance to the Juan de Fuca Strait. There they would turn east toward their destination, Port Gamble, Washington. But the dark night, a shroud of fog, and a full-on winter fury had rendered the *Puritan*, her captain and crew blind and lost. They were at the mercy of an ocean that was not living up to its name — on this night, the Pacific was not the peaceable one.

At the sight of a flash of surging white froth off the starboard bow, a frantic shout rang out above the storm: "Breakers ahead!" But it was too late. The *Puritan* was driven ashore on Bonilla Point. With a terrifying shudder, her hull ripped open on the jagged reefs. The *Puritan* was firmly aground in the Graveyard of the Pacific.

As the seas pummelled her, the *Puritan* lurched on the reef and began to keel over, exposing her decks to the breaking waves. Captain Atwood did not call to lower the lifeboats. There was no point in the men abandoning ship into the void of the starless night. Who knew what lay between the wrecked ship and shore?

The possibility of being swept overboard became all too real as the waves began to wash over the deck. To avoid this fate, the frantic crew scrambled across the sloping decks toward the masts, where they lashed themselves to the rigging. For hours, while the *Puritan* rocked and beat herself against the reef, the men reassured one another and prayed, waiting for the storm's subsidence and the coming dawn.

At first light, the men saw that they were about 300 metres from the beach. But the expanse between the ship and the shore was a shallow reef, awash with the sea's fury. The crew's only chance of survival was to get a lifeline to shore. Once a line was secured, they could rig up a bosun's chair, which the men could then use to sling themselves off the ruined ship. But there was no way to get a man safely ashore. The *Puritan*'s lifeboats had been lost in the night, and only a man with a death wish would try to wade or swim to shore. What the crew of the *Puritan* needed was a miracle.

To the shipwrecked crew looking desperately toward the shore, the final resting place of the *Puritan* must have seemed deserted. A dark, dense forest that looked impenetrable framed the shoreline. How could salvation ever come in such a desolate place? But salvation did come. As the crew considered their futile options for escape, a man came into sight paddling a canoe through the breakers toward them.

Jimmy Nytom, from the local Ditidaht people,

had been fishing in the area when he spotted the wrecked schooner in the distance. With skill that came with a lifetime of living and travelling along this stretch of coastline, he navigated his canoe through the surf and across the foaming reef. But try as he might, he could not manoeuvre his canoe close enough to the ship to take a line from the crew.

Reluctantly, Jimmy had to return to shore, but he did not give up. After waiting for the tide to drop slightly, he swam and waded through the frigid surf out onto the reef as close as he could to the *Puritan* and unwound a piece of fishing line weighted at one end with a stone. As the waves crashed around him, Jimmy began tossing the line to the men on the wreck. If he could get a line aboard the ship, the crew could feed him a stronger line, which Jimmy could then secure to the shore.

In theory, it was simple, but in practice, it was torturous. The distance between Jimmy and the ship was far enough that most of his throws fell frustratingly short. Other attempts that seemed hopefully close were churned aside by the sea. The surf washed over Jimmy, repeatedly knocking him down on the jagged rocks, but still he persisted. Hour after hour, he threw his line while the *Puritan*'s crew tried to grapple the line with a fishhook. While the 10 crewmen could spell one another off, Jimmy was alone at his task. For more than six hours, he persisted until, finally, bruised, freezing, and exhausted, Jimmy threw a line that met and took hold with a line from the *Puritan.*

While the hopeful crew watched, Jimmy waded back to the shore and fastened the line to a spur of jutting rock. A lifeline was quickly rigged, and all the men were safely slung to shore one by one. Jimmy led the exhausted men to a nearby cabin, where they huddled together throughout the night, snatching sleep and keeping warm as best they could.

The next morning, when the survivors looked out to where their ship had foundered, all the masts were gone — consumed by the sea and storm. The *Puritan* lay on her side as waves surged over her. In a few days, the *Puritan* would be completely gone from sight, her remains scattered on the ocean floor.

Fortunately, the wreck of the *Puritan* had also been seen by Thomas Daykin. Thomas was the son of W. P. Daykin, the light keeper at Carmanah Point lighthouse, which was just up the coastline from where the *Puritan* went aground. Thomas hiked to the wreck site and led the crew back to the lighthouse. Although the senior Daykin alerted a passing ship to stop and take on the shipwrecked crew, the ship ignored his request and carried on down the coast, much to Daykin's disgust.

To get the crew safely back to Victoria, Thomas had to take matters into his own hands. He loaded the men in the lighthouse's whaleboat, essentially a sturdy, oversized rowboat, and rowed and sailed the whaleboat south, a journey of about 110 kilometres along the same stretch of water in which the *Puritan* had just been wrecked. Eighteen hours after leaving Carmanah Point, Thomas rowed the *Puritan*'s survivors into Victoria Harbour.

For their heroic efforts, both Jimmy (referred to only as an "Indian" in early accounts) and Thomas were lauded in newspaper accounts. In the dramatic rescue of the *Puritan*, the crew would have perished were it not for Jimmy's persistence — they were but one shipwrecked crew that owed their lives to the Native peoples who lived along Vancouver Island's west coast.

Chapter 2
Honeymoon on the High Seas

I n 1786, Frances Hornby Trevor emerged from a French convent school at the age of 17. Freed from the cloistered environment where she'd spent the last three years, her first stop was to visit her father, the Reverend Doctor John Trevor, at his home in the Flemish port of Ostend. Her visit proved fortuitous, for a chance meeting there with a young sea captain secured a place for Frances in the history of British Columbia.

While Frances visited with her father and enjoyed the freedom of life outside convent walls,

27-year-old Charles Barkley was overseeing the finishing touches on a British trading vessel in a River Thames shipyard. The ship was being outfitted for a private fur-trading venture to the northeast coast of the Pacific. Charles and his backers wanted to capitalize on the new trade in "soft gold," the luxurious pelts of sea otter that could fetch princely sums in Asia. Charles was commissioned to undertake three voyages to North America and China in an expedition that could take up to 10 years.

On September 8, 1786, Charles rode the outgoing tide down the Thames and crossed the Strait of Dover to Ostend. There, he supervised the loading of food and water onto the ship, oversaw the crew, and gathered items for trade, but Charles also found time to catch the eye of a striking young lady with a cloud of golden-red hair. Despite his hectic schedule and the societal constraints for a young woman of the day, Frances and Charles, whether by chance or design, met. A whirlwind courtship followed, culminating in their marriage on October 27, 1786.

A few weeks after their marriage, Charles was due to set sail. But Frances was not willing to let her new husband away without her — their life together had barely begun. So instead of staying in Ostend with her father or returning to other family in

England, Frances chose to accompany her husband. Although she may not have been the first woman to travel with her husband at sea, her decision was courageous for the day. After Frances's years in the convent, her marriage and the upcoming journey presented a most exciting opportunity. She was young, newlywed, and childless. There was little keeping her ashore, so she chose to experience the hardship and excitement of a voyage at sea with her new husband. "I made up my mind to brave every danger rather than separate," Frances later wrote.

Frances was true to her word. On November 24, not even a month after being married, she stood on the deck of Charles's ship, the *Imperial Eagle*, waving goodbye to her family and friends. The mooring lines were released, and the ship set off toward Cape Horn.

Frances's voyage was a daring step for a young woman in the late 18th century. Navigation at the time was part experience, part gut feeling at best, and conditions were harsh. Ships were cramped and rat-infested, food preservation methods primitive, fresh water suspect and unreliable, and both ship and crew were at the mercy of the weather and the temperament of the people they met along the way. Sailors could be afflicted by any of a number of menacing diseases, including scurvy, dysentery, tuberculosis, and small pox. Frances was not setting out on a pleasure cruise.

Soon into their journey, Frances found herself nursing her new husband. Charles caught rheumatic fever and was so severely ill that Frances feared he might not recover. With Charles temporarily incapacitated and out of command of the ship, Frances became the target of unwanted advances from the first mate, Henry Folger. In her reminiscences, Frances mentioned Folger's "unprincipled attention," but did not elaborate. Whatever Folger's indiscretion, Frances apparently dealt with it, making no further mention of his misbehaviour.

Frances nursed Charles through this illness so that he was well enough to resume command of the ship and direct it into Salvadore, Brazil, in early January 1787. Initially, their time in this port of call was unsettling — Brazilian authorities assumed the *Imperial Eagle* was a military ship because of her 20 guns and the officers in naval uniform. But once Charles convinced officials that the *Imperial Eagle* was on a voyage of trade and discovery, the relationship changed. Frances and Charles were invited to social engagements on shore and entertained on board as well. However, their time in Salvadore was short, and on February 7, the *Imperial Eagle* weighed anchor and continued south toward Cape Horn, one of the most notoriously dangerous stretches for sailing ships.

Day after relentless day, the *Imperial Eagle* fought against high winds as it pounded around the cape. From her cabin, Frances could hear the chaos on the deck above as the crew tacked the ship back and forth, often going kilometres off a direct course to make agonizingly slow progress into the headwinds. Below deck, anything not secured was strewn around the lurching ship. Frances occupied herself as best she could in her small cabin until the ship was finally around the horn, sailing away from the dreaded passage.

Although Frances had her wish to be close to her beloved husband, her days at sea were uncomfortable and often numbingly repetitive. Everyone, even the captain and his young wife, was subject to the same stench, cramped conditions, uncertain seas, navigational hazards, and tedium. Food was limited at best, perhaps rotten or full of weevils at worst. Fresh water was severely rationed, and no one was safe from illness, disease, or even death. But Frances seemed to take the discomfort in her stride. Nowhere in the diary she kept during her voyage, nor in the reminiscences she penned in her 60s, did she dwell on her personal discomfort or illness.

As the *Imperial Eagle* sailed north toward the equator, the spirits of the Barkleys and the ship's crew rose along with the temperature. Stores of fresh fruit, meat, and water were happily taken on in Hawaii — it had been three months since the ship had left Salvadore, and fresh food had long since run out. On this brief stop, Frances also acquired a female companion, a maid called Wineé. Now she had someone with whom to pass the days on board.

From Hawaii, the *Imperial Eagle* set out to the northwest coast of North America to acquire the cargo that was to fuel the Barkleys' voyages. Frances and Charles were riding the wave of the era's lucrative maritime fur trade. The frenzy for sea otter pelts was initiated primarily by Captain James Cook. In 1778, Cook landed at the native village of Yuquot, in Nootka Sound, on the west coast of what is now Vancouver Island. He remained in the village for a month, trading weapons, tools, and "fancy clothes" for food, artwork, and furs, including sea otter pelts. Although Cook was killed a few months later in Hawaii, his crew sold the sea otter furs in China for impressive sums, thus igniting the European sea otter trade in the northeast Pacific.

By the mid-1780s, the "soft gold" rush was on.

Yuquot quickly became a key port of call for traders seeking the luxurious pelts in exchange for metal and other highly prized objects. British, French, Spanish, and American vessels all descended on this small stretch of the coast. Between 1785 and 1805, nearly 50 trading expeditions arrived at Nootka Sound. Frances and Charles's arrival in June 1787 was one of these voyages.

* * *

Frances watched from the deck, her red hair swirling around her, as canoes approached the Imperial Eagle. Each of the large canoes, carved from cedar trees, held several Mowachaht men, clad in furs, skins, or wraps made of woven cedar bark. The men greeted the Imperial Eagle with gestures and in a language that was unintelligible to the Barkleys and the crew, but the Europeans recognized the encouragement for the ship to follow the canoes. The Mowachaht men led the Imperial Eagle to a broad open bay in a protective moorage that Europeans had named Friendly Cove.

While the Mowachaht people had seen many foreign vessels, this was the first ship they had seen with a woman on board. In fact, on this trip, both Frances and Wineé found their way into the history books: Frances as the first European woman and Wineé as the first Hawaiian, male or female, to visit the northwest coast of North America.

One of the first visitors that Charles and Frances received on board the *Imperial Eagle* created quite a stir. Shortly after the ship had moored, a canoe came alongside the *Imperial Eagle* and a man who looked very much like a Native person from the village came on board. To their surprise, the man spoke English and identified himself as Dr. John MacKay, a surgeon off the trading brig *Captain Cook*. MacKay had been living among the people of Yuquot for almost a year, having been left there to recover from purple fever. (His captain had promised him a voyage home in the next year or so.) Frances wrote that he was clothed in a greasy sea otter skin and was very dirty, and that his habits and customs were "disgusting."

Regardless of how off-putting his appearance was to Frances, MacKay proved to be a valuable friend to the Barkleys. Having learned the language of the local people, he worked as a translator for Charles. As Charles had the Nootka Sound trade to himself for the first part of the *Imperial Eagle*'s stopover, MacKay assisted him in securing successful transactions. Soon, the *Imperial Eagle*'s holds were filled with a cargo of sea otter pelts.

However, Charles found himself getting mired in the politics of England when two other British ships, the *Prince of Wales* commanded by Captain Colnett and the sloop *Princess Royal* commanded by Captain Duncan, arrived. The crews of both ships were extremely sick with scurvy, having left London 10 months before. At first, relations between the captains and crews were friendly, particularly because Charles supplied the ships with fresh deer meat and other much-desired goods (including wine and brandy). But when the new arrivals realized Charles had monopolized most of the trade, leaving the Mowachaht people willing to trade only for copper — of which the *Prince of Wales* and the *Princess Royal* had none — the relationship began to sour. Tension mounted because Colnett also suspected that Charles was operating illegally in the area. Colnett's assumption was correct.

The ship that Charles had sailed down the River Thames and over to Ostend was called the *Loudoun*. However, when the young captain and his new bride had sailed from Ostend 10 weeks later, they were sailing the *Imperial Eagle* — but the ships were one and the same. Charles and his financial backers had changed the name and hoisted Austrian colours before setting out. At the time, British ships trading on the northwest coast of North America needed to procure a licence from the East India Company. By outfitting the ship in a foreign port and changing the vessel's name and flag, Charles and his partners avoided paying for the costly licence.

In an attempt to uncover the ruse, Colnett sent his first mate on board the *Imperial Eagle* with a letter demanding that Charles produce papers proving authority to trade in the region. Charles instead tried to flummox the man by showing him letters and papers in a language he couldn't understand. As far as Colnett was concerned, the fact that Charles and most of the crew were British was proof enough of deceit, and he decided to pursue the *Imperial Eagle*'s illegal trade back in England.

Perhaps sensing the rising tension, Charles determined it was time to leave Nootka Sound. On July 24, 1787, shortly after the awkward exchange with Colnett's mate, the *Imperial Eagle* sailed from Yuquot with 800 sea otter pelts secure in its hold. It was on this southbound journey that Frances and Charles left their mark on the southwest coast of Vancouver Island. A day or two after leaving Yuquot, Charles pulled out his inkwell and quill and commenced naming several locations on this coastline, believing himself to be the first person, European at least, to closely examine this stretch of shore.

To a large sound, Charles bestowed his own name. In honour of his bride, he named Frances Island and Hornby Peak. Other landmarks were named after the crew, including Cape Beale after the *Imperial Eagle's* purser, John Beale. (On today's charts, only Barkley Sound and Cape Beale, as well as the names of the three main channels separating clusters of islands in Barkley Sound — Imperial Eagle Channel, Loudoun Channel, and Trevor Channel — remain as reminders of their journey. Others named these channels, and Folger Island, long after the Barkleys' journey.)

Rather than sailing directly to Asia, Charles elected to conduct more trade with Native peoples as he sailed down the coast of North America. At one stop, just past the Strait of Juan de Fuca in Washington State, six men went ashore seeking Native peoples interested in trade, but they never returned. The next day, a well-armed search party found only bloodied clothing and scraps of linen. Almost immediately, Charles and his devastated crew decided to leave the North American coast. But before sailing to China, he named the river where the tragedy occurred Destruction River.

The *Imperial Eagle* sailed into the port of Macao

in December 1787. After making a profit of more than $25,000 on the otter skins, Charles proceeded to Mauritius in the Indian Ocean and then on to Calcutta, where he was to provision for his second voyage. However, it was here that Charles lost command of the *Imperial Eagle*. In a move that embittered the Barkleys, and which Frances never forgave or forgot, Charles's backers sold the *Imperial Eagle* and all its contents, including charts, nautical instruments, and other provisions Charles had paid for, out from under him. The illegal trade of the *Imperial Eagle* in Nootka Sound had been uncovered, and Charles's associates were anxious to distance themselves from the expedition.

Charles eventually sued his associates and was awarded more than $12,000 before the case went to court. However, he had expected to be busy trading on this route for 10 years, and now found himself without a ship or a job. To add insult to injury, Charles's possessions, including his journal, were transferred to Captain John Meares of the East India Company. Meares went back to trade on the northwest coast of North America, and it is believed that he passed off several of Charles's discoveries and achievements as his own when he published his journals. Frances was incensed, writing in her diary:

"Capt. Meares ... with the greatest effrontery, published and claimed the merit of my husband's discoveries therein contained, besides inventing lies of the most revolting nature tending to vilify the person he thus pilfered." Charles never wrote about his own expeditions, and this was likely part of the impetus that spurred Frances to record her reminiscences later in life. She was determined not to let her husband's name and achievements be lost from history.

While they were in Mauritius, Charles and Frances's first child, William Hippolyte, was born. With Charles having lost his ship, the young family stayed with friends in Mauritius until they gained passage on an American ship bound for England. But even the trip home was not without incident. Within sight of England, the boat wrecked but stayed afloat long enough for the passengers to be rescued thanks to the floatation of its cargo, a load of cotton. Frances wrote, "My beloved husband, myself and one infant son ... found ourselves alone on the wreck the morning of the night she struck, the vile captain and his crew having deserted us and the ship in the night." The Barkleys eventually made it to Portsmouth on November 12, 1789, on an English ship. Frances was just 20 years old, and her first, and longest, voyage with Charles was over.

Despite the abrupt end to Charles's contract, the young family crisscrossed the globe many more times, travelling between England and Mauritius, Calcutta, Siberia, Alaska, and New York on other trading voyages, during which they experienced many adventures, yet also endured personal tragedy.

Less than two years after their return from Mauritius, the Barkleys were en route to Calcutta. During this voyage, their second child, Martha (Patty) was born during a violent gale off the Cape of Good Hope. It was also during this voyage that Charles again became seriously ill with what Frances called a "violent colic." The sight of her husband in excruciating pain and in convulsions frightened Frances but, as she had before, she stoically nursed him back to health.

Tragically, the same disease claimed their beloved Patty, who died one day shy of her first birthday. An anguished Frances kept her child in a leaden box until the ship could land to bury her. Her dear Patty was buried in a coconut grove on one of the Spice Islands. Frances found some solace in the fact that her infant was buried in what she felt was one of the most beautiful places in the world.

Frances and Charles sailed on six voyages together, with only periodic breaks ashore, from November

1786 to November 1794. These voyages saw Frances become the first Englishwoman to visit Hawaii, British Columbia, and Alaska. From November 1794 on, however, Frances remained ashore. She had five more children, although William Hippolyte died at 14 years of age and a second boy, also called William, died as an infant.

Frances and Charles corresponded throughout his subsequent voyages and, to the last letter, were always affectionate and loving with each other. Charles would write to "His ever Dear Love, Fanny" and signed letters with phrases such as "God for ever bless you, the best of women ..."

Frances kept busy with children and then grandchildren. Then, in 1832, she sadly recorded in her diary that "On May 16 I lost my beloved husband, — in his 73rd year — worn out more by care and sorrow than by years, as he had been blessed with a very strong constitution." In 1835, Frances began to write her reminiscences, likely feeling it was important to recognize Charles for his achievements and voyages, as Meares, Cook, and others had been.

With Charles gone, Frances took quill in hand. By recording her thoughts and remembrances, Frances was also bringing to light her own remarkable achievements. At a time when society had very explicit ideas about the role of young women, Frances Barkley challenged those ideas with strength and courage.

Chapter 3
Life on the Lights

Lighthouse keepers have played a crucial role in British Columbia's maritime history. Despite the isolation and often appalling working conditions, the keepers did their best to keep lights flashing and foghorns sounding on a coastline that brought peril to so many.

The light keeper's presence gave reassurance and relief to countless mariners. The flash of a light in a raging storm or the blast of a horn resounding through a featureless wall of fog prevented many ships from being chronicled as yet another victim of the Graveyard of the Pacific. Light keepers also assisted shipwreck survivors, offering shelter and sometimes even transporting them to Victoria. Lighthouse keepers and their families are truly the unsung heroes of the southwest coast. Here are the stories of two such families.

* * *

It was the evening of Boxing Day 1901 and a fearful squall was pummelling Vancouver Island's west coast. Through it all, the keeper of Carmanah Point lighthouse, William P. Daykin, then a 10-year veteran of this remote posting, had to ensure the constant operation of the flashing beacon atop the light tower. Its regular pulse of light across the ocean alerted any mariners caught in the maelstrom to the island's looming presence. The steam boilers that powered the whistle and foghorn seemed forever greedy for coal. Every few hours, William climbed the light tower to crank up the counterweights that kept the light turning.

In the morning, the storm's wreckage littered the light station grounds. All the fences were down, the spikes that held the flagpole's guy wires fast had been pulled up, hundreds of trees had toppled in the forest, and two windows in the house had been blown out. Farther down the coast, a steamer's distress whistle sounded along the desolate shore. Its cry ultimately went unanswered — there was no way to reach or contact the endangered vessel. Later, one of William's sons found butter casks, a schooner's rudder, broken oars, and a shattered raft strewn along the shore. There was no mention of any survivors in the lighthouse log.

William Daykin was a legendary light keeper along Vancouver Island's southwest coast. While stationed at Carmanah Point lighthouse, a rocky promontory close to the middle of the Graveyard of the Pacific, he filled nine volumes of journals, leaving one of the most detailed first-hand accounts of life on West Coast lighthouses.

William Daykin arrived at Carmanah Point lighthouse on April 17, 1891, with his wife, mother, and five sons. From that day, he chronicled the weather, the comings and goings of ships past his post, shipwrecks, and other notes about life on the lights. William also frequently wrote about his frustrations with lack of support from Victoria and from the supply ships that, in his estimation, were often neglectful in their ability to supply the station. His jottings were filled with descriptions of the seemingly endless rain and storms. References to rotten coal, filthy oil, and

Carmanah Point lighthouse

faulty equipment were also frequent.

The constant dickering with coal and oil, the light and foghorn, meant that William's sleep — when he could catch some — was often interrupted. When the machinery broke down, he had to tinker with it until it was operational since replacement parts could take months to arrive. Several times during his tenure at Carmanah, William had to crank the light by hand through the night to keep it revolving when gear wore out. The inferior oil constantly charred the wicks and fouled up the windows on the light. William wrote: "Wound lamp and trimmed wicks every night, will soon have to trim wicks twice a night." The charred lamp wicks covered the light's lens in soot, and William spent hours cleaning the prisms and windows. It was a relentless job.

While keeping the light operational was of utmost importance, William was also responsible for maintaining the fog alarm. That the fog alarm was steam driven would explain William's rantings about inferior coal and the ravenous nature of the boilers, as well as the constant dampness in the station's buildings. His frustrations were poured into the daily log: "4 pm started signal — had to stop few minutes at 5 to clean grate — very poor coal." The frequent shipments of poor-quality coal plagued William as he continually had to shut down the boiler to dump the grates and scour the tubes with a wire brush.

The boilers also operated a steam whistle used to communicate between ships and the lighthouse. Using an international code of signals relayed by flags (during the day) or steam whistle blasts (at night or when visibility was poor), William sent and received messages from passing ships.

In theory, Carmanah Point lighthouse was a telegraph station as well as a signal station. William was the intermediary in communication between ships and Victoria or Port Alberni. Vessels signalled William, who was then to relay messages along the coast via a crude telegraph line. But the telegraph system was little more than a wire strung between posts or tree branches, and storms often brought branches or trees down on the line, rendering it useless. This meant that William, or one of his sons, spent much of their time tending the line, with the hope that it would be operational when needed. Too often, however, the line was down, often for weeks, sometimes months, adding another frustration to William's growing list of complaints.

Despite the diligence of William and other light keepers on the coast, tragedies occurred. Foul weather, a perilous shoreline, and crude navigation methods claimed victims, but William and his family were always prepared to assist shipwrecked mariners. They kept provisions on the station for survivors and attempted to get word out of the fate of wrecked ships and their crew via the telegraph or, if that failed, by signalling passing ships. If help did not come in a timely manner, William or his sons often transported the survivors to Victoria themselves using the station's whaleboat. In more tragic situations, it was the Daykins who patrolled the shoreline looking for wreckage and even bodies.

William's journals were peppered with complaints about the lack of supplies getting to the lighthouse in a timely manner. While stormy weather often prevented safe offloading, William whipped himself into a frenzy watching the supply ships pass the light in fine weather, without stopping to offload his mail, pay, or supplies, including fresh meat and liquor. He wrote that one time the *Quadra*, the government lighthouse tender, had been in sight of the lighthouse. When it became clear the ship was not going to stop, William hired a Native man to paddle out to the boat. "... [A]lthough the canoe was within 200 yds of the *Quadra*, they would not stop. Fired 3 shots but they took no notice ..." Even when supplies were successfully landed, they were often wet or ruined. In one instance, a supply ship landed almost 20 kilograms of spoiled meat that had been on board for more than a month. William recorded: "The meat was alive ... sent it back on board."

The hardship of life at Carmanah Point lighthouse took its toll on William and his family. He lost his first wife and two sons. When she was ill, his wife was taken to Victoria, but William's pleas to be moved to a closer posting were denied and Mrs. Daykin died in hospital alone. One son was killed as he rode down a freight trolley car that ran from the lighthouse to the beach below. The son was killed instantly when the cable snapped, throwing the 17-year-old to the beach below. A second son died while out hunting with a friend. Their canoe was discovered floating and fully loaded on a nearby lake, but neither boy was ever found.

The stress of life on the lights gnawed away at William's health. The constant cold and damp left him crippled and in pain with arthritis. In the end, his vocation might even have robbed him of his sanity.

In early lighthouses, the heavy lenses in the light tower floated in a tub filled with mercury. One of a lighthouse keeper's duties was to drain the mercury from the tub and strain it through a cloth. During this maintenance, it's possible that the keeper could absorb some of the deadly metal through his skin and lungs. The poison could then make its way to the body's central nervous system, including the brain — symptoms of mercury poisoning can include rheumatism, dementia, and emotional instability. Whether this close contact with mercury contributed to William's poor health will never be known, but near the end of his time at Carmanah Point, his shaky journal entries seemed ever more cryptic and disordered, with mystifying references to "Keno" peppering the journals. "Good night, Keno—where ever you are," reads one.

By 1912, more than 20 years of interrupted sleep, inadequate housing, and the stress of arguing with superiors had taken its toll. For many of his years at Carmanah Point, William had begged to be taken off the post and transferred elsewhere. Eventually, in March, his request was honoured and he was moved to MacLaughlin Point near the entrance to Victoria Harbour, where he died four years later. William had spent 21 years at Carmanah Point lighthouse — his replacement lasted only six weeks.

* * *

In the 1860s, Emmanuel Cox, his wife Frances, and their infant son and two daughters joined the throngs leaving Ireland for new opportunities and fresh hope in America. Prior to leaving Ireland, Cox had been an overseer on the estates of Lord Hamilton, in county Cork, and much to the consternation of her parents, Frances became infatuated with Emmanuel. Frances's parents had hoped she would wed Lord Hamilton's son and heir and, in a society obsessed with class, felt that her choice of husband was a misguided one.

To escape the restraint of family and class, the Coxes emigrated first to California and then booked passage north for Esquimalt, on the outskirts of Victoria. Emmanuel found work as a farm labourer and began to eke out a meagre living. During this time, the governor general of Canada, Lord Dufferin, visited Victoria. Lady Dufferin was the daughter of Lord Hamilton and sought out the Coxes to renew acquaintance with people she knew from the "old country." Concerned about the Cox family's poverty, Lady Dufferin persuaded her husband to exert his power to find Emmanuel a position within the civil service.

On March 8, 1876, Emmanuel was appointed light keeper at Berens Island lighthouse, at the entrance to Victoria Harbour. Despite their hopes for an improved life, the posting was difficult for the growing family, which now included five children. The pay was poor and the living conditions cramped — the lower floor of the family's quarters measured only 3 x 4 metres, while the upstairs bedroom was little more than an oversized closet. After almost two years, Emmanuel applied for, and received, a promotion. The family was again on the move, this time north to the remote western shore of Vancouver Island and Cape Beale lighthouse.

Early in 1878, Emmanuel, Frances, and their children, Frances, Annie, Pattie, Charles (Gus), and Ernest (Ruxton), headed to Cape Beale. Since getting all but the smallest vessels close to Cape Beale lighthouse was difficult even in good weather, the family was deposited at Dodger Cove on Diana Island in Barkley Sound. There, the young family boarded with the storekeeper for a week, waiting for the weather to break so they could make it to their new home.

When the weather calmed, the family and their belongings were loaded into five canoes, each with three local native men to paddle them to the lighthouse. The journey meant crossing a wide stretch of open water, but their guides were expert at handling the small crafts, and the Coxes quickly realized they could have had no better, more experienced guides.

While paddling toward Cape Beale, the group had an unexpected and terrifying escort. A pod of killer whales broke the surface around them, their sleek bodies coming so close that their wash rocked the canoes. Black fins sliced the surface, and the puffs from the whales' exhalations hung like clouds of liquid jewels above the water before dissipating. The children later recounted the experience as being frightening, but their guides soon had them laughing as they landed the canoes through the surf. Then, one by one, the men slung the Coxes onto their backs — including 90 kilogram Emmanuel — carried them through the breakers, and deposited them on the beach.

Their safe delivery to their new home was the beginning of the Cox family's strong relationship with the local Native peoples of Barkley Sound during their long tenure at Cape Beale. They relied in particular on one man, John Mack, paying him $5 per month to be ready to assist the family. When they needed him, they hoisted the Union Jack and John would paddle over from Dodger Cove.

As with most lighthouses, contact with the outside world was limited. Steamers called into Dodger Cove only two or three times a year with mail and supplies for the Coxes. Aside from shipwrecked mariners, few visitors ever went to the station. Should a message need to be sent, the Coxes engaged John or another man to deliver it by canoe to a passing ship. He even paddled to Victoria. Snippets of world news trickled into the station from passing ships and the sporadic mail. The Coxes, in landing on this wind-blasted rock in the Pacific, had got their wish in spades to escape the rigid society they'd left in Ireland.

Most ships passing Cape Beale were bound to or from the Juan de Fuca Strait. Other vessels might turn into Barkley Sound, heading for trading posts in the region, such as the one at Dodger Cove. Before venturing near the strait, ships often had to wait for good conditions and could be seen offshore from Cape Beale lighthouse waiting for a tug or good sailing weather. At times, there were as many as 10 ships offshore. Cox's logbook entries recorded the reality of maritime travel of the day: "19 June 1879. Large barque at 1:30 west, bearing in direction of lighthouse. Passed lighthouse steering north. Must have mistaken Barkley Sound for Juan de Fuca Strait. Sea fog coming in, got very close to rocks here. Saved herself by throwing anchor."

Although they were technically not employees, a light keeper's family, including his children, often took an active part in the station's maintenance.

Staples were brought on supply runs, but everyone had a role to play in gathering, growing, and preserving food, and in the day-to-day chores of maintaining a family of seven in such an isolated location.

The family's work often extended to the operation of station safety equipment as well. One day, young Frances Cox went into the wooden light tower to begin her daily chore of winding a weight around a drum that kept the light mechanism turning, much like the springs and cogs in a grandfather clock. But Frances forgot to insert a peg that held the weight in place before she began to wind and watched in horror as the weight crashed to the bottom of the well, far out of reach for anyone at the lighthouse. With Emmanuel away, Frances, her siblings, and her mother had to hand-crank the light at a steady speed to keep its flash across the sea synchronous with what mariners expected from their charts. They did this for 10 nights from dusk until dawn. Finally, Emmanuel returned with the part needed to repair the light and the nightly vigil ceased.

For the Cox daughters in particular, life at Cape Beale handed them a chance to experience adventure and independence that they likely would not have been afforded in society off the lights. On one occasion, in 1890, Pattie was in charge of the station when she saw a fully rigged ship, the *Old Kensington*, becalmed off Cape Beale and drifting dangerously close to the rocks. Pattie wired Victoria, asking for a tug, but none would come without a security of $500. Having no way to contact the ship, Pattie provided the guarantee for the ship herself, and the tug arrived the following day to tow the *Old Kensington* to safety. Months later, Pattie received a parcel from China, with a note from the ship's captain, a silk shawl, 2 kilograms of tea, and a photograph of the *Old Kensington* under full sail.

Annie and Pattie also had fond memories of another experience. The supply ship *Sir James Douglas* called at the light only twice a year, so visitors were few and far between. One year, however, a sealing captain landed his wife at Cape Beale to visit with Mrs. Cox and the children while he went to work on the sealing grounds. On the return trip, Annie and Pattie eagerly accepted the captain's offer of a trip to Victoria, thinking they would return on the *Sir James Douglas*. But after enjoying their time in the city, and preparing to return home, the sisters discovered that the tender was out of commission. This meant that the girls might have to wait for weeks, perhaps months, for a trip home.

Life on the Lights

Unfazed, the sisters met a native couple they knew from Barkley Sound and paddled home with them in their canoe. Each night on the four-day journey, the girls helped haul the canoe out of the water, assisted with the fire and cooking, then wrapped themselves in blankets and settled in for the night under a tree or other shelter.

The Cox children drifted off the lights as they left for school, jobs, and marriage. Emmanuel died at Cape Beale in 1894, leaving Frances to sadly raise the Union Jack and summon John from Dodger Cove once more to help her relay the news to her children. Several months later, despite her attempts to be kept on as light keeper, Frances also left Cape Beale, her home for the past 16 years.

* * *

The Daykins and the Coxes provide a glimpse into the life of early families on the lighthouses of the southwest coast of Vancouver Island. Despite the hardship, especially that endured by the earliest keepers, the allure of life on the lights has persisted, and Carmanah and Cape Beale, as well as Pachena, constructed between the other two in 1908, continue to be staffed, often by keepers with young families.

Chapter 4
Coastal Lifeline

Hundreds of pioneers journeyed to the west coast of Vancouver Island with high hopes for a new life. But living conditions were not easy, and only a handful survived the harsh environment. Those that stayed eked a living from the land or took one of the few jobs that existed, such as maintaining the telegraph lines that were strung along west coast shores.

A Lineman's Life
In 1894, David and Sarah Logan boarded the coastal

vessel *Maude* with their 11-month-old son, destined for a place they had never seen, to take care of a herd of cattle and a small homestead for a man they hardly knew. The Logans were leaving Victoria, heading north to the native village of Clo-oose, on the southwest coast of Vancouver Island. As they neared their destination, the steamer slowed but did not drop her anchor. Several canoes, paddled by villagers from Clo-oose, manoeuvred alongside the ship to assist the Logans ashore.

After offloading their gear on the beach, the young couple watched the *Maude* steam away. Their homestead was still about a kilometre away, they had few possessions and a tiny babe, and they were probably as isolated as they had ever been. If the Logans had any reservations, however, this was not the time to question their decision. Shouldering their gear, the young family turned and hiked through the rainforest, along the banks of the Cheewhat River toward a simple cabin and the river flats where the cattle grazed.

The Logans had arrived on Vancouver Island's west coast because of a chance meeting in Victoria with a man named G. F. Groves. In 1892, Groves had purchased land near Clo-oose and built a house on the upper reaches of the Cheewhat River, a meandering tidal river permanently stained the colour of tea by the tannins in the cedar-infused soil. Here, in the hummocky grass flats, Groves and his wife raised a herd of cattle. But the couple stayed for only two years, before returning to their homeland, Australia, after convincing David to look after their property.

Born in Scotland in 1864, David Logan emigrated to the eastern seaboard of the United States, then moved to Illinois to work in the mines. There he met Sarah Usher, also a new immigrant to America. They later went to Victoria, via California, where David, like many Scots, found employment in the flourishing coal mine industry. While in Victoria, the Logans met the Groves, who proposed a chance at pioneering life. The Groves never returned to Clo-oose, but the Logans lived there for the rest of their lives.

The Logans had arrived in a place that was very sparsely inhabited. There were native villages nearby, including the one at Clo-oose, and the Cox family lived up the coast at Cape Beale lighthouse. But with none of a city's amenities, and limited means to travel and communicate with others, the Logans had to rely on their wit and ingenuity to survive and keep themselves safe, sane, and healthy. Life could be lonely and harsh — the region was wet and often storm-swept. But the land was also incredibly bountiful and stunningly beautiful. Determined and resourceful, the Logans rose to the challenge of making a life on this rugged shore.

To generate some income, David and Sarah made butter, which they shipped to Victoria by coastal steamer. They also sold meat, but instead of receiving cash from their purchaser, they sometimes traded for bundles of second-hand clothing. After two years of living near the river, during which time they lost a child in infancy, the Logans moved to a store that Groves had built at the east end of Clo-oose Bay.

A few years before the Logans arrived at Clo-oose, government wheels in Victoria had been set in motion to develop a communication system between the lighthouse at Cape Beale and Victoria. At the time, the only way the light keepers at Cape Beale could get word of a maritime disaster "out" (or request personal supplies and equipment to repair and service the light) was to hire a local Native person to paddle the coast with a message for officials in Victoria — hardly a timely means of averting tragedies or assisting shipwrecked mariners. Construction of the telegraph line between Victoria, Cape Beale, and Bamfield was complete by 1891. With the Logans now living at Clo-oose, David was ideally positioned to work at maintaining the line and was hired to patrol the section between Clo-oose and Cape Beale.

A lineman's job was to follow the rough track, muddy and riddled with slippery tree roots, to ensure the telegraph line — a single strand of galvanized wire strung from tree to tree — was intact and to remove any branches or trees that were impeding transmission. Given the frequency of high winds on this storm-lashed shore, it was a merciless job. David was sometimes away for weeks tending to the line. He'd no sooner get it working when another storm would batter the coast and he'd have to begin his trek over again.

David proved to be ideal for the job. He was fit and resourceful, and quickly adapted to coastal travel in a place where tides shifted throughout the day and rivers regularly swelled and changed course throughout the winter. He often walked the trail without shoes and didn't bother with waterproof clothing. To cross streams and rivers, which could vary from a trickle to a torrent, David waded or used canoes that were stashed on the banks. Other times, he'd crash through the bush along the banks of the stream, often going far upstream and off his route to search for a narrower crossing or a suitable log that spanned the reach.

While he was away tending the line, David

carried some light provisions, but also lived off the land and sea. He took shelter in caves, native smoke-houses, and crude shelters he'd constructed from driftwood and ships' wreckage deposited on the beach. While the shelters offered some respite from the weather, they were far from cosy. David's son Bill recounted that on a trip he took as a child with his father they bedded down on mats woven from reeds. Sleep that night proved elusive, however, as they were kept awake by the incessant attention of fleas.

David lived at Clo-oose until his death in 1938, 44 years after he stepped off the *Maude* and into a waiting canoe that would take him to shore. During his days there, he assisted many shipwrecked mariners and slogged along the rugged, muddy trail to keep the telegraph line intact. He also served as postmaster and justice of the peace. Many of the Logans' children remained at Clo-oose for years, including son Bill, who also became a lineman, and daughter Sarah, who married a lineman. The Logan name lives on in the region, at Logan Creek south of Carmanah Point lighthouse.

The Wreck of the *Vesta*

Although the telegraph line that David Logan worked hard to maintain was meant to permit communication, in reality, it was so often interrupted by fallen trees and branches that it was of limited use. Nonetheless, many shipwrecked mariners owe their lives to the work of David and the other early linemen. They kept the telegraph lines open as best they could and went to the assistance of mariners when they heard about wrecks. This sometimes meant having to slog through the night, their surroundings illuminated only by the glow of a miner's lamp, to reach the wreck, where they'd assist survivors or recover bodies.

The very presence of the telegraph line and the linemen's shelters along it also resulted in the survival of some shipwrecked survivors. People who survived the terror of a wreck often found themselves on a desolate shore with only two options for escape: the pounding sea before them or the seemingly impenetrable forest behind. If they weren't lucky enough to be seen and rescued by Native people, light keepers, or linemen, this was their reality. The sight of a piece of wire slung between the trees and a crude trail through the rainforest provided a glimmer of hope in a desperate situation. The wreck of the *Vesta* was one such time when the presence of the telegraph line helped survivors find their way to safety.

The schooner *Vesta* was en route from Huenema,

California, to Port Townsend, Washington, when she missed the entrance to the Strait of Juan de Fuca due to rough seas and poor visibility. Soon, she was off course and foundering in the high seas. On the morning of December 9, 1897, the *Vesta* was lifted by a monstrous wave and driven over the reef west of Carmanah Point, where she was carried up into the edge of the forest and wrecked. The *Vesta* was high and dry in the coastal rainforest.

All eight crew members had survived the wreck and now set about securing their survival and rescue. Within a short time of exploring their surroundings, they found the telegraph line, which they followed until they got to a signpost indicating their exact bearings and the distance to Carmanah Point lighthouse. Deciding against travelling farther down the rugged, muddy trail to the lighthouse 14 kilometres away, especially since the weather was still dreadful, the crew made camp at the wreck. Two days later, the weather had improved enough for the captain and four men to set off for Carmanah Point lighthouse, where light keeper W. P. Daykin and his family welcomed them. After taking a much-needed rest, the men returned to the *Vesta* with Daykin's son Thomas to get the rest of the crew.

While the presence of the telegraph line had

helped the survivors find assistance, the line was interrupted because of the storm, so the Daykins had no way to contact Victoria. They would have to take the shipwrecked crew to Victoria themselves. Thomas launched the lighthouse whaleboat, loaded the *Vesta*'s crew, and set off toward Victoria. But before long, the weather deteriorated and gale-force winds were tossing their open boat. As wave after wave crashed over the boat, threatening to swamp it, the desperate crew bailed furiously.

By now, almost a week after the wreck, ships passing the *Vesta* had realized her fate. Would-be rescuers had spoken to a man guarding the wreckage and learned that the crew and Thomas had set out for Victoria on the evening of December 14. But they were long overdue — the 110 kilometre trip should have taken less than a day. Headlines in the December 17 issue of the Victoria Colonist read "Where Is the *Vesta*'s Crew?"

But the strong wind and high seas prevented Thomas and the *Vesta* crew from running down the Strait of Juan de Fuca into Victoria. Instead, they had run across to the American side of the strait to Neah Bay, where Thomas deposited the crew, who proceeded to Seattle.

When interviewed later, Thomas described the

wreck as being so damaged and deep into the forest that no high tide would likely ever refloat her: "She is standing high and dry and you could plant potatoes inside her." Indeed, the *Vesta* did stay in the forest and David Logan often used her as a cabin when he was repairing the telegraph line. Years later, when all metal fastening and salvageable parts had been removed, the *Vesta* was burned. While the tangible remains of the *Vesta* were gone, her story as ship and shelter, for mariners and linemen, survives.

Chapter 5
Putting Bamfield on the Map

At the close of the 19th century, the community of Bamfield was a tiny coastal village, a safe harbour for fishing boats, and home to the Huu-ay-aht people and a few of the coast's early traders and settlers. The small village clustered around two inlets and was tucked inside Barkley Sound, just around the coast from storm-whipped Cape Beale. Bamfield might have remained remote and relatively unheard of were it not for the fact that the community became an unlikely, yet strategic, location in the around-the-world communications network of Britain and its colonies.

The idea of a telegraph link closely associated with the cross-Canada railway had been talked about for several decades. As early as 1863, Sir Sandford Fleming, railway surveyor and chief engineer of the Canadian government, had proposed an all-British telegraph route that would first cross Canada to the Pacific, then continue by submarine cable to Australia and New Zealand. It would connect the transatlantic route that had already linked Europe with the United States and Canada in 1866.

Prior to the invention of telegraphy and its subsequent perfection in the 1840s, overseas messages were transported physically via ships. Reporters or government officials greeted ships at the docks and disseminated news via the press or word of mouth. Telegraphy changed this cumbersome system by making it possible to create electrical messages that could be transmitted over great distances in minutes. Generated by tapping Morse code with a telegraph key, the code's dots and dashes were translated into electrical impulses that were transmitted over submarine or above-ground telegraph cables.

In the late 19th century, the British Empire was at the height of its power. British cartographers of the day traditionally coloured the British colonies red on world maps, and the completion of the round-the-world telegraph link was integral to the British desire to have an all-British telegraph route — an "All Red Route" — encircling the globe. The completion of the railway, the technology of telegraphy, and the push for an All Red Route all came together to put the tiny community of Bamfield on the map.

On September 13, 1886, the Canadian Pacific Trans-Canada Telegraph System was completed, with telegraph lines running parallel to the Canadian Pacific Railway lines, from the Atlantic to the Pacific. To achieve an All Red Route that encircled the globe, all that remained was the link across the Pacific. However, it took 14 years for this last link in the telegraph system to become a priority. Finally, in March 1901, the *Quadra* left Victoria to scout a location for the Canadian terminus of the cable. In addition to having favourable ocean floor topography and few obstacles for the submarine cable, the location had to be far from heavy shipping traffic so that boats' electrical signals (not to mention their anchors) would not interfere with the functioning of the telegraph cable.

In the end, Bamfield filled this criteria best. It was about as far west as one could get, without being

too far from Vancouver and Victoria. Coastal steamers regularly travelled near the village from Victoria
and also down the Alberni Canal from Port Alberni.
Bamfield was isolated, pristine, and quiet, but not
too much so.

The final task of laying the route across the
Pacific Ocean was no easy feat to accomplish. Prior to
laying the cable, the ocean floor had to be surveyed
to determine ocean depth and topography — the
cable needed to follow the contours of the ocean
floor and could not be draped from peak to peak of
underwater mounts. To determine a suitable deep-
sea route, the cable ship *Brittania* began to survey
the Pacific's seabed in August 1901.

From the survey, it was determined that the next
stop after Bamfield in the All Red Route would be
Fanning Island. This barren atoll in the mid-Pacific is
about 6400 kilometres from Bamfield, approximately
the distance from Victoria to Halifax. From Fanning
Island, the cable route would extend to Fiji, Norfolk
Island, and then on to Southport, Australia, with
a spur to Doubtless Bay, New Zealand. From
Southport, the route continued by land to Sydney.
The laying of the thick cable began in September
1902, with the custom-built 7250 tonne *Colonia* (no
existing ships could carry the incredible length of

cable required) paying out cable from Bamfield to Fanning Island. Another ship, the *Anglia*, started in Southport, working toward Norfolk Island and then on to Fiji and Fanning Island. The 6400 kilometres of cable laid from Bamfield to Fanning Island still holds the record for the longest continuous stretch of underwater cable in the world.

On October 31, 1902, the last piece of cable was laid and the Pacific section of the worldwide link was completed. To mark the occasion, a celebration was held in Victoria. A large map of the All Red Route was prominently displayed and telegraphic equipment was set up, with operators exchanging congratulatory messages from all over the world. Sandford Fleming sent the first "world-circling telegraph message" on the same day: "To Governor General, Ottawa: Receive globe encircling message via England, South Africa, Australia and Pacific Cable congratulating Canada and the Empire on completion of the first segment state controlled electric girdle the harbinger of incalculable advantages, national and general. From Ottawa, Oct. 31, 1902 Sandford Fleming."

With the completion of the All Red Route, messages now took only minutes instead of days, or even months, to be delivered. The original cable could

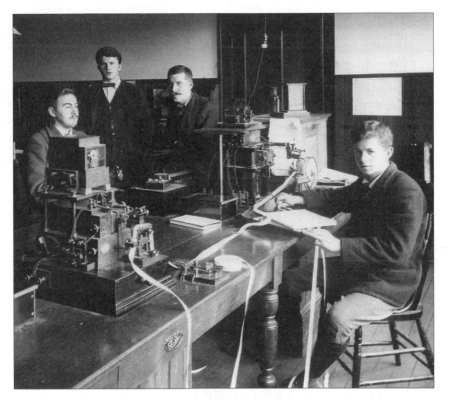

Telegraph operators at Bamfield Cable Station

send about 110 letters per minute, but eventually the speed was increased to 135. Still, it took skilled telegraph operators to send, receive, and interpret messages.

One of those operators was R. Bruce Scott, who steamed into Bamfield Inlet on the *Princess Maquinna* in the spring of 1930. Although he was only 25, Bruce was a veteran of other cable stations in the Pacific system, and had worked in Australia, New Zealand, Fiji, and Fanning Island.

When the *Maquinna* rounded the corner into Bamfield Inlet, Bruce and the other passengers were greeted by a charming chateau-like residence with a commanding view over Barkley Sound. The striking building was designed by one of the most fashionable architects of the day, Francis Mawson Rattenbury, whose commissions included BC legislative buildings and Victoria's Empress Hotel. When it was completed in 1902, the building was the grandest in town. A manager's residence and bungalows for married men and other assorted outbuildings completed the assemblage. In 1926, when a second cable was laid along the same route, a three-storey concrete building was built on the cliff face below the Rattenbury building. Bruce said this building resembled a "Tibetan lamasery," but noted that other men, particularly lonely bachelors, called it Alcatraz.

Despite the area's remoteness and the community's small size, for those willing to make the best of their situation, Bamfield offered unending opportunities. The village had a stunning ocean location, with lakes and rivers for fishing, trails for hiking, and beaches for exploring. Bruce was obviously suited to west coast life — within an hour of his arrival, he had strapped on his boots and was hiking the trails along the coast.

With no road connecting Bamfield to the outside world, its two inlets became the "main streets" of town — to get almost anywhere meant using a boat. Bruce aptly described the town as a west coast Venice, recalling ladies heading to parties with their evening gowns protected by "waterproof slickers, sou'-easters and gumboots." They would arrive "at the dance hall, or a friend's house … [and] each would emerge from her rain-clothes like a butterfly from a chrysalis, resplendent in the latest fashion."

Life at the cable station offered a variety of activities for the employees: a billiard room, a library with 3000 books and an open fireplace, a music room, and a large dining room with a spectacular view. Scott referred to the station's "country club-like" life, with outdoor pursuits of tennis, boating, fishing, swimming, hiking, and hunting always a possibility. There was a staff orchestra and regular dances, remarkably well timed for the arrival of the coastal steamer, the *Princess Maquinna,* when she took a five- or six-hour stopover from nine in the evening to the wee hours of the morning. Bruce and other bachelors, "clad in flannels and blazer," would meet the *Princess Maquinna* on the northbound route and give "the girls the once over as they came down the gangplank with a view to making a date for the dance on the return trip." It was at one of these dances in 1941 that Bruce met his future wife, Pauline. After dancing with Bruce for most of the evening, Pauline left on the *Princess Maquinna* at three in the morning, but the two continued to correspond. The next year, she came for a holiday and they were married the year after that.

Although life in Bamfield offered many activities and opportunities for the cable station employees and their families, workdays were long and often tedious — but not without pressure. An operator was allowed only one error every 7000 words while transmitting and receiving messages. If this was not achieved over a year, the operator lost his annual pay increment and was fined.

However, there were also periods of great excitement and tension. During World War I, Royal Engineers from Victoria were sent to Bamfield to protect the station from sabotage and attack. Within days of their arrival, barbed wire surrounded the station and people had to pass through a guarded entry. Staff worked 12-hour shifts seven days a week due to the large volume of messages. When the Germans cut the cables at Fanning Island, Bamfield operators had a short respite from the exhausting work before the line was fixed.

Bruce was at Bamfield when World War II was declared. Again the barbed wire and sentries appeared and the cables were jammed with messages. Censors worked with the cable operators to decode and record all messages. For six years, the cable operators' workdays were long, and rest and relaxation time all too short. There was little time for dances and the other social occasions the community so enjoyed.

Bamfield became a critical relay station during this war after the Italians cut the cables in the Mediterranean Sea in 1940. This disruption in the round-the-world cable meant that messages sent from the battlefront in Africa to London had to be routed via the Indian Ocean, Australia, through to Bamfield, across Canada, and finally to London via the Atlantic cable. Bruce remembered one foreboding message sent by a news correspondent describing the fall of Singapore. His final message, on February 11, 1942, read "Now closing down. Most unlikely able to evacuate. Please inform wires. Goodbye."

Not all messages that travelled along the cables were quite so grim. During the war, Bruce sent a message along an old stretch of cable that ran to Victoria asking the operator at the terminus to call the hospital to inquire as to the condition of Pauline, who was awaiting their birth of their first child. Not long afterward, Bruce received a cable: "It's a girl! Both doing well."

Up until 1956, about 45 people worked at the Bamfield Cable Station, but their time would soon come to an end. The service was becoming increasingly automated, requiring fewer men on each shift. As well, the above-ground stretch of cable that ran from Bamfield to Port Alberni was the most unreliable link in the communications system. From Bamfield, a copper cable ran above ground, often strung from tree to tree, to Port Alberni and Parksville. As this line was frequently interrupted, officials decided to replace it with an underground cable linking the Pacific cable directly to Alberni, bypassing Bamfield. In 1959, the new submarine cable was laid up the Alberni Inlet and the Bamfield station was closed. Bruce remained an employee until the end. The last message sent from the Bamfield Cable Station was on June 20, 1959. It read "Farewell from Bamfield before closing down after fifty-seven years of operation and leaving it to the shades of the past."

Chapter 6
The *Valencia* Tragedy

On January 23, 1906, readers of a special edition of Victoria's *Colonist* newspaper were met with the headline "S.S. VALENCIA WRECKED NEAR CAPE BEALE." The subhead went on "Between 50 and 60 Lives Lost — Pathetic Scenes Aboard: 125 Persons Still on Vessel With Death Staring Them In The Face."

As people read this, the *Valencia* was still being ravaged by high seas. Passengers were desperately clinging to the ship's rigging or huddling near the wheelhouse between crates of cabbages. A life raft with four poor souls was drifting toward Turret Island in Barkley Sound, some of its passengers slipping into insanity en route, haunted by the mental and physical torture of their ordeal. Before the day was out, the wreck of the *Valencia* would go down in the sea. It would also go down in the history books as the BC coast's worst maritime disaster. By the time the last survivors were rescued, at least 117 people had died. Stories of the tragedy of the *Valencia* reverberated along the west coast for years.

The passenger ship *Valencia*'s last run departed San Francisco on January 20, 1906. The trip began like many others. Crews prepared the ship for departure, stoking the steamer's firebox and readying to release mooring lines. Passengers in their fine travel clothes walked up the canvas-sided gangplank and gathered at the rails to wave to friends and family. As the ship pulled away, the captain, O. M. Johnson, emerged from the wheelhouse to look up at his daughter and wife waving goodbye from their apartment overlooking Meiggs Wharf. The ship's whistle blew and the *Valencia* was off, bound for Victoria and Seattle.

The trip started out well, with fair seas and fine weather. Nothing seemed out of the ordinary and, all going well, the ship was scheduled to reach the entrance to the Strait of Juan de Fuca sometime around midnight on her third day out to sea. The passengers amused themselves reading, playing games, and relaxing on the deck, in their cabins, or in the saloon.

Near Cape Mendocino, the weather began to sock in, and fog enveloped the steamer. Captain Johnson started to navigate by a system of dead reckoning. He tracked the time and the *Valencia's* speed using a patent log, a propeller-like device towed behind the ship that registers the distance travelled through the water. To calculate the ship's position, the captain used the time and distance travelled along a particular magnetic bearing. Johnson also ordered the occasional sounding to calculate depth, which he compared against his chart.

This method of navigation is part skill and experience, and part instinct. The patent log readings can vary given the sea conditions and current direction, resulting in less than exact readings. (Confusing readings can result because the log is not necessarily being towed straight out behind the ship. Rather, due to currents and rough seas, it could travel back and forth, resulting in distorted measurements.) If Johnson had taken a regular series of soundings, he would have had more precise information. But he didn't do this and he failed to account for current speed and sea conditions when reading the patent log. Johnson and the *Valencia* were unknowingly almost 60 kilometres off course.

On the evening of January 21, Johnson estimated they were approaching Cape Flattery and the entrance to the Juan de Fuca Strait, which would lead them to Victoria. Reducing the ship's speed, he ordered his men to begin throwing lead lines over the side to determine depth. Johnson knew that if the ship was close to schedule, it should soon be passing over the shallow Umatilla Reef. The crew started throwing lead overboard, but from 6:00 pm to 9:30 pm, no depth was recorded — the ocean was deeper than the lines could reach. According to the second officer, Peter Petterson, it was recorded in the log that 240 fathoms (432 metres) of lead line had been cast out, although no bottom was found. The winds and sea had been building throughout the day and, by now, the ship was beginning to pitch. Meanwhile, passengers were no doubt looking forward to their arrival in Victoria, which was scheduled around breakfast the next morning.

Still assuming he was south of Cape Flattery and approaching Umatilla Reef, Johnson calculated a new bearing, slightly east of their position. According to Petterson, Johnson stated that he thought the pilot log was "over-running" (recording a distance greater than they had actually travelled) because of the current's influence, and therefore he thought they were still about 60 kilometres south of the Umatilla lightship that marked the reef. In fact, the pilot log was probably recording a distance *shorter* than the ship had travelled because they were going *with* a strong northerly current — they were probably just off the Umatilla lightship, or perhaps even to the north of it.

Soundings continued to be taken. At 9:30 pm, there was a sounding of 80 fathoms; at 10:00 pm, 60 fathoms was below the *Valencia* — if the ship was, as Johnson thought, nearing the mouth of the Juan de Fuca Strait, the readings should have started to read 150 fathoms or more. A perplexed Johnson ordered the ship to move at half speed. At 10:30, the sounding was 60 fathoms; at 10:45, 80 fathoms; at 11:00, 60 fathoms again.

Now the ship travelled dead slow, and the storm rose around the anxious crew. Johnson and his officers stood by, listening for leadsmen's readings and any other sounds that would help determine their location. The soundings became progressively shallower and more unsettling: 56 fathoms at 11:15, 33 fathoms at 11:30. If the *Valencia* was on course, she should have been in water much deeper than 60 metres. Suddenly Petterson saw a dark object ahead where there should have been nothing but sky. "By God!" Captain Johnson exclaimed, "where are we?" He ordered a course hard to starboard and Petterson took over the helm just as "24 fathoms" was shouted into the darkness. Johnson lunged for the telegraph arm to ring "full stop" when he was thrown off his feet as the ship struck a reef.

The *Valencia* was nowhere near Cape Flattery or the entrance to the Juan de Fuca Strait. Rather, she had gone aground about 16 kilometres north of Carmanah Point lighthouse — becoming another victim of the Graveyard of the Pacific. In desperation to get off the rocks, Johnson signalled the ship's engine room to go full astern. The *Valencia* had not gone hard ashore, and after a few agonizing seconds, with the sea and wind whipping foam and spray around, the *Valencia* scraped free and backed off the rocks.

But before Johnson could breathe a sigh of relief, his engine room crew scrambled up on deck, having been flushed out by rapidly rising seawater coming from a hole in the bow. Johnson had only one choice — to drive the ship back onto the rocks to stop it from sinking in deep water. He signalled to the engine room for full speed ahead, and the *Valencia* shuddered forward, coming to a full, grinding stop on the reef.

As the *Valencia*'s lights cut through the wafts of fog and blackness, Johnson and his crew began to get a glimpse of where they were. They were fast on a rock only about 30 metres from a cliff face that rose far above the ship's funnel. The *Valencia* was at rest in the sea's breakers, fully exposed to open ocean swells. Waves washed the deck and exploded against the hull and the reef around them. Wind and sleet swirled around the doomed ship as passengers and crew scrambled onto the deck. Topside cargo, including crates of cabbages, littered the deck. One crew member recounted the scene: "Screams of men, women and children mingled in awful chorus with the shriek of the wind, the dash of the rain, and the roar of the breakers. As the passengers rushed on deck, they were carried away in bunches by huge waves that seemed as high as the ship's mastheads. The ship began to break up almost at once and the women and children were lashed to the rigging above the reach of the sea. It was a pitiful sight to see frail women, wearing only night dresses, with bare feet on frozen ratlines, trying to shield children in their arms from icy wind and rain."

The Valencia *Tragedy*

Johnson quickly ordered the lifeboats to be lowered to the rails and lashed in place. Within half an
hour, at least four, perhaps five, lifeboats were hap-
hazardly lowered and launched — with disastrous
results. One smashed against the *Valencia*. Others
launched unevenly, tipping the passengers — mostly
women and children — into the surf. One boat successfully made it to the sea, and the people on deck
watched as the oarsmen struggled to pull the boat
through the boiling surf, trying to keep it too from
being crushed against the *Valencia*. Crewman Frank
Lehm wrote of the desperation: "We all thought them
saved when suddenly a great breaker, larger than any
I had ever seen, aided by a terrible gust of wind,
struck the [life]boat, slewing her around in spite of all
that the man at the steering oar and the sailors could
do. The next moment she was overturned. What a
sight! The searchlight showed every detail of the terrible tragedy — the men and women struggling in the
water, their faces ghastly in the glare; eyes that stared
at us unseeingly, already glazed with the touch of
death; the bodies of children swept toward the terrible rocks, in a wild chaos of boiling surf. Suddenly all
of this vanished, the searchlight revealing only a tossing, rolling, terrifying rush of water."

Within 30 minutes of the *Valencia* hitting the

reef, 40 to 60 passengers and crew were dead. To add to the terror of those on board, the rising waters extinguished the ship's lights, casting the ship into utter darkness.

During the night, people on board the *Valencia* clung to the rigging and cowered in the stern, huddling together under the tarpaulins and taking shelter as best they could in the lee of the wheelhouse and between the crates. The crew tried to calm and comfort the survivors, providing blankets and food. Johnson fired distress rockets, losing two fingers in the process. Bed clothing, linen, and even ladies' skirts were soaked in kerosene and burned to hail any nearby ships.

As daylight approached, the people on the ship could better assess their situation. The shore was frustratingly close — as one officer later testified: "[It] was so handy, you could almost take an orange and throw it on the cobbles on the shore ..." Yet devastation met the survivors in every direction. Carnage was all around them. Bodies hung from the rigging and floated around the ship amid the crates and cabbages and other debris. More corpses surged back and forth against the shore, slowly being scoured of their flesh as they rubbed on the rocks.

Of the dozens of people who had clambered into

the lifeboats just after the *Valencia* wrecked, only 12 made it to shore alive. Nine of them disappeared into the forest, but passengers still clinging to the ship were somewhat cheered when they saw three survivors on shore. Their hopes turned to horror though as they watched the men attempt to scale the sheer cliff face, where they were trapped by the rising tide, only to watch as one, then the next, then the next, slipped and fell to his death on the rocks and booming surf below.

At daylight, Johnson organized the launch of a lifeboat to take a group ashore and try to secure a line that he would fire from a Lyle gun. This line could then pull up a heavier line that could be used to sling passengers off the ship. The handful of crew, which included boatswain Tim McCarthy, launched the lifeboat and desperately pulled away from the ship, travelling north to avoid landing at the base of the cliffs. The current took the men farther than expected, however, and after five hours of rowing and drifting, they landed at a small sandy beach. Exhausted, the men waded ashore and battled through the underbrush, desperate to find help. Eventually they came upon a weather-beaten cabin at the edge of the forest. On the cabin was a sign that read "3 miles to Cape Beale."

Back on board the *Valencia*, Johnson tried to use the Lyle gun to carry a line to shore. The line on the first shell frayed and broke, but the second line went high over the top of the cliff. The crew watched and waited, hoping that one of the crew that they assumed had made it to shore by now would secure the line. (By then, the men from the lifeboat launched that morning were probably in the parlour at Cape Beale lighthouse.) But after a few hours, the survivors on the ship watched in horror as the rope, which had chafed through, slid over the cliff and into the water. Their last projectile had been used to fire that line, and as it slithered into the sea, another hope for rescue was dashed.

When McCarthy and the crew stumbled into the yard at Cape Beale lighthouse, they were met by Minnie and Tom Paterson. And when the Patersons exclaimed that they must be the men from the shipwreck, the crew was shocked. The nine men who had disappeared into the forest after making it ashore the night before had reached Minnie via telegraph as they huddled in a lineman's cabin at the Darling River. Minnie in turn had relayed news of the shipwreck to Victoria.

After learning that the men in her yard were not the ones she'd already spoken to, Minnie assumed that the men in the hut might need assistance. She immediately tried to contact them on the line. Once they'd reconnected, through a very crackly wire, she instructed them how to tighten the loose wires. After a better connection had been established, one of the men told her that the nine in the shelter were in very bad shape. Minnie assured them she would send for help and then contacted the light keeper at Carmanah Point, W. P. Daykin. Along with telegraph linemen David Logan and Joe Martin, Daykin began a long trek north to assist the shipwrecked men in the shelter and to see if they could help those still on board the ship.

On the *Valencia*, almost 100 people still clung to the hope that help would arrive, but time was quickly running out. The ship was beginning to break up. Survivors were climbing the ratlines and mast to get as far away as possible from the surf raging below. Getting a line ashore was still seen as the only hope, but since no men had appeared on shore to secure a line, the only way to do this was to get a line from ship to shore themselves.

John Cigalos, one of the *Valencia's* firemen, volunteered for the task. Tying a rope around his waist, he dropped into the frothing sea. After trying for more than half an hour to swim through the breakers while wood and debris surged around him, Cigalos was hauled back on board exhausted. He recounted his ordeal: "I cross myself, I say Good-bye, boys. I jump overboard and swim hard through the surf … sea was full of sticks, boxes, and everything; so I try to swim, slack the line and so a big sea wash me back, I dove under so I was very close but I can't catch my hands because too much suction, it was me out again … a big stick, heavy stick, hit me on the head so I get headache at that time, I looses my senses enough, so I take my knife and get it off right away … I try to get to shore again, but the sea so rough, if I cut the line to go out myself I might go but I was sorry for the other people, if I lose, I lose myself, if I am alive every body all alive, I do not want to be alive myself, and I am sorry, so any way I can't land myself."

(Cigalos was later rewarded for his bravery with $100 gathered from the First Methodist Church in Seattle and a medal that was inscribed "He did his best.")

The passengers on the *Valencia* had to endure another terrifying night on board the dying ship. As dawn broke, their situation looked futile — the ship was in its death throes and no help seemed imminent. The sea was still high and the ship continued to break up and settle deeper into the sea, forcing the

John Cigalos, survivor of the Valencia.

shivering survivors farther into the rigging or the top of the wheelhouse.

But unbeknownst to them, ships were en route thanks to Minnie's telegraph to Victoria. At about 9:30 that morning, one ship appeared on the horizon, then another. A cheer went up on the deck — perhaps there was hope after all. Johnson fired the Lyle gun three times to alert the ships, and crew and passengers in the rigging frantically signalled for help.

At about 10:00 am, Daykin, Logan, and Martin made it to the cliff above the *Valencia* after a punishing 18-hour trek through the night. They had located the wreck when they saw a line across the trail — the other end of the line shot from the Lyle gun. The men followed it to the cliff edge and peered through the salal bushes to the ghastly scene below. When they appeared, they too were hailed by those still on deck. Unfortunately, the men could do little other than watch the scene unfold before them.

From their vantage point on the cliff, Daykin could see the ships standing off the *Valencia*. The *Queen City* and the tug *Czar* had arrived from Victoria. The *Czar* moved in toward the *Valencia* and located its position. Remarkably, the captain of the *Czar* reported to the *Queen City* that he did not see any survivors. After going alongside to relay the position of the wreck to the *Queen City*'s captain, the *Czar* steamed away, much to the horror of those clinging to the rigging on the *Valencia.*

Later, the *Queen City* steamed toward the *Valencia* and the captain reported seeing first two masts, then a funnel, and then about 30 people swaying from the rigging, with more gathered around the stern. By 11:00, the *City of Topeka* had also arrived. All the vessels ran as close as they dared to the wreck, but none put down a boat. Presumably they felt that the fate of the *Valencia*'s lifeboats would be their own if they ventured too far into the enormous seas.

In a final denouement, the survivors watched the *Queen City* steam away. The *City of Topeku* was from the same line as both the *Valencia* and the *Queen City*, the Pacific Coast Steamship Company, and she carried on board the company's manager. For reasons never disclosed, the manager ordered the *Queen City* to leave the scene, probably believing that all hands on board the *Valencia* were, or shortly would be, lost.

It was clear that the *Valencia* was not going to last much longer. Captain Johnson realized that their one remaining hope was to put people in the two inflatable life rafts left on board. After pleading with some of the women to get in the rafts, who all refused, Johnson loaded them with male passengers and crew: 10 in the first raft and 17 in the second. After successfully launching the rafts, Johnson joined those who remained on deck, about 70 or 80 people, as they sang "Nearer My God to Thee." Daykin, Logan, and Martin watched the desolate scene while the hymn wafted up to them.

Shortly after, a final thundering wave struck the *Valencia,* breaking it and spilling the survivors into the sea. The men on the cliff could see people clinging to bits of the ship's wreckage, but most were swept out to sea. None that they could see made it to shore. Deliverance from the slow torture the survivors had endured for almost two days had finally come.

After the rafts had been launched, the first raft moved away quickly from the ship and was soon out of sight. The men on the second raft rowed desperately to get out of the surf, every stroke a struggle. As they surged up and down the swells, they heard the *Queen City* blow her whistle four times, a final salute before she steamed off. From the crest of the waves, they could see the *City of Topeka* on the horizon, about a kilometre away. When they were finally free of the breakers and in open ocean, the men hoisted a man to their shoulders and he raised a makeshift flag from an oar.

The Valencia *Tragedy*

Crew on the *City of Topeka* eventually spotted the raft and changed course toward it. After watching it for a while, however, a crew member determined it was just flotsam and the ship resumed its previous course. But soon the *Topeka*'s captain went up on deck and, after watching the bobbing wreckage, was astounded to see there were survivors on board. The *City of Topeka* made for the raft and launched a lifeboat to mercifully tow in the *Valencia*'s life raft, which was now filling with water and beginning to sink. A survivor from the raft related: "We were almost paralysed with cold, for the water had been washing over us for several hours and we had drifted about five miles from the wreck. Some of the men were mostly in the water, while others did their best to keep them from washing away ..."

After the men in the second life raft were rescued, the *City of Topeka* began to search for the first raft. The ship moved in ever-widening circles, scanning for hours through the area, before presuming all were lost. Some of the men in the first raft had died, but not all of them. This raft had drifted into Barkley Sound, well out of the search area. The men were exhausted. Each shouldered an unimaginable weight of grief that began to work away at his sanity. Reports on this raft's survivors vary. Some say that men died

as it drifted to Turret Island and were pushed overboard to make room for the living. Other accounts
say that one man, perhaps more, became distraught
and inconsolable and jumped overboard as the raft
drifted. Another enraged man tried to strangle a fel-
low passenger. The four survivors, including one rav-
ing man found clinging to a tree, were rescued from
Turret Island by local Native people and taken to
Cape Beale lighthouse.

At the end of the ordeal, the survivors who made
it ashore, and those that were rescued by the *City of
Topeka*, totalled 38. No women or children survived.

The next chapter of the *Valencia* tragedy was
played out in newspapers and government inquiries.
Newspapers across North America reported on
the tragedy with headlines announcing "APALLING
DISASTER" and "WHOLESALE MURDER." Serious
navigational errors were deemed to have caused the
disaster, but human behaviour — including the
action, or inaction, of the ships that went to aid the
Valencia and the inability of the men on shore to
assist the ship — was also called into question.

As inquiries continued in Seattle and Victoria,
Logan and others, including some survivors of the
Valencia who returned to help, had the grisly task of
looking for bodies along the coastline. Logan's son

recounted that his father went temporarily blind after completing the numbing and grim task. A freight shed in Bamfield became an impromptu morgue where bodies or partial remains were stored until they could be taken to the city. Many people were never found.

For years afterward, there were stories of a ghost ship that patrolled the coastline near the wreck of the *Valencia*. A report in the *Seattle Times* said that sailors swore they had seen a phantom ship "that resembled the ill-fated *Valencia* … and that they could vaguely see human forms clinging to her mast and rigging." Another recounted that a native man and his wife had come upon a lifeboat in a sea cave that contained eight skeletons. W. P. Daykin from Carmanah Point lighthouse sent his sons to investigate, but they could not get into the cave because of the relentless surf.

One story that can be substantiated, however, is that of the *Valencia*'s Lifeboat No. 5. In 1933, 27 years after the *Valencia* disaster, the lifeboat was found *intact* in Barkley Sound. Its nameplate is now in Victoria's Maritime Museum, the only tangible remains of the ill-fated steamer's last trip.

* * *

One of the recommendations of the inquiries that followed was to improve navigational aids along Canada's west coast. These included a new lighthouse and foghorn at Pachena Point, near the site of the wreck, and the installation of lifeboats at Bamfield. As well, a report recommended upgrading the existing trail that ran along the telegraph line from Port San Juan to Cape Beale. This included fully provisioned huts with working wireless sets every 10 kilometres. The "lifesaving" trail was to be patrolled by a full-time lineman at least once a day, regardless of the weather. The Pachena Point light station was completed in 1908, and work began on the West Coast Lifesaving Trail (or Shipwrecked Mariner's Trail) in the spring of 1907. This route is now called the West Coast Trail, a hiking trail in Pacific Rim National Park Reserve.

Chapter 7
Rescue of the *Coloma*

On December 6, 1906, the barque *Coloma* was towed down the Juan de Fuca Strait and out to sea. The ship was heavily laden with lumber and bound for San Diego. Released by the tug off the entrance to the strait, she set her sails to meet the rising breeze. The wind continued to increase, blowing harder and harder until it reached gale force. The *Coloma* began to labour, hampered by the strain of the cargo on her deck and in her holds. During the night, the lumber on deck broke free in the storm and was swept over the sides, taking the ship's gunwales with it.

The ship was now helpless and breaking up, the mainmast being first to fall. Soon the hull began to take on water and the vessel started to settle until her decks were fully awash. There was little the crew could do — even the lifeboats had been wrecked. In desperation, the crew clung to the rigging. Captain Allison would later say, "[The crew] looked death in the face. At one time we didn't expect to live another 15 seconds."

In the early morning hours, the crew saw that the ship was heading for the rocks, but fortunately they were also right below Cape Beale lighthouse. The captain hoisted the international distress signal, an upside-down flag, to alert Tom and Minnie Paterson, the keepers at Cape Beale, should there be any question the crew was in peril.

From their perch on the bluff, the Patersons could do little to help. They had no lifesaving equipment, and the telegraph line to Bamfield, about 8 kilometres away, was down. The one hope was to somehow get word out. The Patersons knew that the *Quadra* was anchored in Bamfield Inlet waiting out the same storm that had destroyed the *Coloma*. Tom couldn't leave as he needed to stay on his post at the lighthouse, so Minnie threw on a sweater and a hat, called to their dog Yarrow, and prepared to leave. On her feet, she wore her husband's slippers, thinking they would be lighter and less cumbersome than boots.

Clutching a lantern to light her way through the dense, dark forest, Minnie scrambled down the steep incline behind the station. Here, she had to surmount the rising tide in a lagoon at the base of the cape. At high tide, the lagoon fills, cutting the station off from the trail to Bamfield. Not wanting to wait for the tide to drop or even to take the time to launch a boat, Minnie lifted her skirts and waded across the lagoon, becoming drenched in the chilly waist-high water before she'd barely begun her trek.

Minnie walked and ran as fast as she could along the rough track, scrambling over fallen trees, and slogging through the mud wallows. When she reached the end of Bamfield Inlet, Minnie looked for a boat to row down the inlet, but the boat usually stashed in the bush was gone. Luckily, the tide was going out, so she was able to scramble along the slippery narrow strip of shoreline that was just emerging at the water's edge. In places where there was not enough shore to walk on, she waded through the water, and when the water was too high, she crawled through the underbrush.

Minnie clawed along the shore for a kilometre or so until she reached the house of James McKay, the lineman who maintained the trail from Bamfield to Port Alberni. James was away but his wife, Annie, was home. What a sight Minnie must have been — drenched and mud-covered, with her hair dripping wet and full of twigs. After Minnie breathlessly blurted out news of the emergency, the two women launched a boat and rowed down the inlet to the *Quadra*. The *Quadra*'s Captain Hackett must have been shocked to see two women frantically rowing toward him through the rain and wind. However, within 10 minutes of Minnie and Annie relaying the *Coloma*'s looming danger, the *Quadra* had lifted anchor and was steaming toward Cape Beale.

By now, the *Coloma* had drifted away from Cape Beale and was laying low in the heavy seas near Seabird Rocks at the entrance to Pachena Bay. All its masts were gone, the sails were torn away, and the bow was split open, spilling more lumber into the swirling seas.

Minnie, meanwhile, after leaving the *Quadra*, rowed on to the Bamfield Cable Station, where she relayed news of the imperilled ship to the station employees. Cable operators quickly sent out word of the disaster to Victoria, while others attended to

Minnie. She gulped the tea the men offered, but declined their suggestions to rest and dry off — Minnie had a nursing baby and four other children back at Cape Beale and was anxious to get home.

Two men from the cable station insisted on accompanying Minnie to the light, and the trio piled into a boat and quickly rowed down Bamfield Inlet. Now that Minnie had temporarily stopped moving, the pain set in. Her legs and stomach knotted with cramps, and the cold seeped deep into her aching bones. By now, Tom's slippers were caked in mud and probably in tatters, but Minnie refused to rest for fear she would be unable to move again. When her legs crumpled under her at Long (Topaltos) Beach, about halfway back to Cape Beale, she told the men she had just stumbled. Picking herself up, Minnie gathered what little strength she had left and carried on, urging the men to hurry along with her.

It was a week before the telegraph cable was repaired and the Patersons knew if Minnie's efforts had been successful. Captain Hackett and the *Quadra* had arrived at the *Coloma* as it was in its final death throes. A lifeboat was lowered off the *Quadra* and took the men off the sinking ship one by one.

The media soon grabbed hold of Minnie's trek and heralded her heroic efforts. The Canadian government presented her with an inscribed silver plate and $50. The Seattle branch of the Sailors' Union of the Pacific presented her with a framed citation recognizing Minnie's "sterling worth as the highest type of womanhood, deeply appreciating her unselfish sacrifices in [on] behalf of those 'who go down to the sea in ships' and assure her and hers of our undying gratitude."

A week after the incident, a newspaper reporter arrived at Cape Beale to meet Minnie. He brought with him a purse with a gold locket and a cheque for $315.15 collected by the ladies of Victoria and Vancouver, a silver tea set from the crew of the *Coloma*, and a new pair of slippers for Tom. Minnie told the reporter about "life on the lights" and how, during the storms, "the spray flies right over the house and the salt gets so thick on the windows you can't see out ... the wind would shake an ordinary house to pieces." She also talked about the other wrecks and tragedies her family had witnessed from their post at Cape Beale, concluding that she would "rather not have the money and the nice things that have been said about me than to have had the wrecks."

Although Minnie received accolades and fame for her epic trip, she paid with her health. After this ordeal, her constitution was never the same. She eventually contracted tuberculosis and died five years later.

Bibliography

Graham, Donald. *Keepers of the Light.* Madeira Park, BC: Harbour Publishing, 1985.

Hill, Beth. *The Remarkable World of Frances Barkley: 1769–1845.* Sidney, BC: Gray's Publishing, 1978.

McMillan, Alan D. *Since the Time of the Transformers: The Ancient Heritage of the Nuu-chah-nulth, Ditidaht, and Makah.* Vancouver: UBC Press, 1999.

Nicholson, George. *Vancouver Island's West Coast 1762–1962.* Victoria: Morriss Printing, 1962.

Scott, R. Bruce. *Barkley Sound: A History of the Pacific Rim National Park Area.* Victoria: Sono Nis Press, 1972.

Scott, R. Bruce. *Breakers Ahead!* Sidney, BC: Review Publishing House, 1970.

Scott, R. Bruce. *Gentlemen on Imperial Service: A Story of the Trans-Pacific Telecommunications Cable.* Victoria: Sono Nis Press, 1994.

Scott, R. Bruce. *People of the Southwest Coast of Vancouver Island.* Victoria: Morriss Printing, 1974.

Wells, R. E. *A Guide to Shipwrecks Along the West Coast Trail.* Victoria: Sono Nis Press, 1981.

Wells, R. E. *There's a Landing Today.* Victoria: Sono Nis Press, 1988.

Acknowledgments

In a book such as this, filled with historical stories about people who are no longer with us, I am blessed to have family and colleagues passionate about the history of my province, and specifically about Vancouver Island. This book would still be in the morass of my computer were it not for my father, David Mason, former archivist at the BC Archives, whose research skills, endless support, and willingness to search for just about anything were a great help. My husband, Bob Hansen, has travelled with me through fog, rain, mud, and, yes, even sunshine, to all the places mentioned in this book. I couldn't have asked for a better companion. My children, Ava and Patrice, are also most cooperative and cheerful about boating, hiking, and generally poking about in all sorts of weather.

For an area that is so sparsely inhabited today, the west coast of Vancouver Island has had a wealth of writing pertaining to it. I am thankful for the foresight of George Nicholson and R. Bruce Scott, who began to research and compile stories about this region more than 30 years ago. Most of their books are out of print, but it's worth the effort to find them in the library or a second-hand bookstore. I would also like to acknowledge the work of Donald Graham, Beth Hill, Richard E. Wells, and Michael Neitzel. Their efforts to sort through letters, journals, and government reports, and to conduct hours and hours of research cannot go without admiration and recognition. Their books and others for those keen on learning more about this region are listed in the bibliography.

I would also like to acknowledge the following sources for the quotes contained in this book: *Gentlemen on Imperial Service*, R. Bruce Scott; *Breakers Ahead!* R. Bruce Scott; *Keepers of the Light*, Donald Graham; *The Valencia Tragedy*, Michael Neitzel; and *The Remarkable World of Frances Barkley: 1769–1845*, Beth Hill.

Finally, many people answered questions, read portions of the manuscript, or provided me with details and resources necessary to complete the work. Thanks to Linda Myres, Bamfield Community School; Andrew Mason, Golder Associates; Allison Cronin, UBC Museum of Anthropology; Silva Johansson and Barry Campbell (Rtd.), Pacific Rim National Park Reserve; Fred Sieber and Alfred Knighton, Ditidaht First Nation; and Jerry and Janet Etzkorn, Carmanah Point lighthouse.

About the Author

Adrienne Mason is a writer, naturalist and life-long resident of Vancouver Island. She enjoys hiking, beachcombing, and exploring the coast with her husband and two daughters.

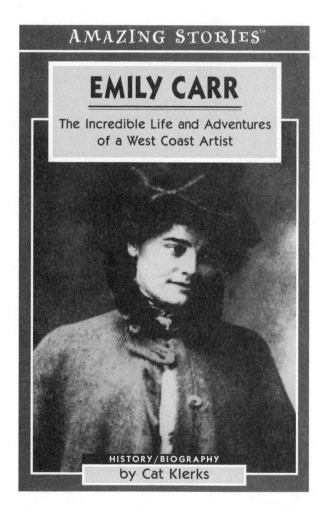

AMAZING STORIES™

EMILY CARR

The Incredible Life and Adventures
of a West Coast Artist

HISTORY/BIOGRAPHY
by Cat Klerks

Emily Carr
ISBN 1-55153-996-9

AMAZING STORIES™

VANCOUVER'S OLD-TIME SCOUNDRELS

Gassy Jack's Exploits and Other Skulduggery

HISTORY/BIOGRAPHY

by Jill Foran

Vancouver's Old-time Scoundrels
ISBN 1-55153-989-6

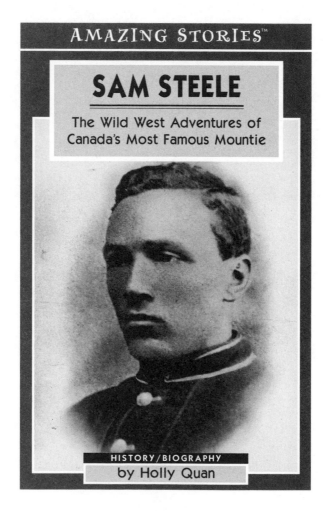

AMAZING STORIES™

SAM STEELE

The Wild West Adventures of
Canada's Most Famous Mountie

HISTORY/BIOGRAPHY

by Holly Quan

Sam Steele
ISBN 1-55153-997-7

AMAZING STORIES™

ROMANCE IN THE ROCKIES

The Lives and Adventures of
Catharine and Peter Whyte

HISTORY/BIOGRAPHY
by Kim Mayberry

Romance in the Rockies
ISBN 1-55153-998-5

Dogs to the Rescue
ISBN 1-55153-995-0

AMAZING STORIES™

HORSE TALES

Heart-warming Stories About
Living With Horses

ANIMAL
by Gayle Bunney

Horse Tales
ISBN 1-55153-994-2

AMAZING STORIES™

MARY SCHÄFFER

An adventurous woman's
exploits in the Canadian Rockies

HISTORY/BIOGRAPHY
by Jill Foran

Mary Schäffer
ISBN 1-55153-999-3

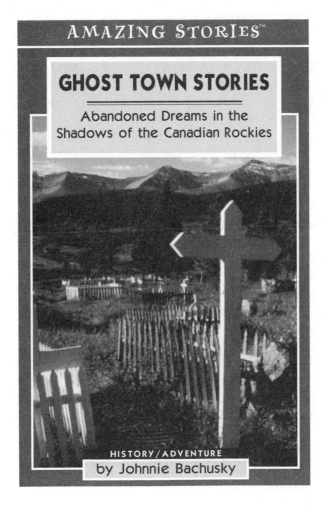

AMAZING STORIES™

GHOST TOWN STORIES

Abandoned Dreams in the
Shadows of the Canadian Rockies

HISTORY/ADVENTURE
by Johnnie Bachusky

Ghost Town Stories
ISBN 1-55153-993-4

OTHER AMAZING STORIES

ISBN	Title	Author
1-55153-977-2	Air Force War Heroes	Cynthia Faryon
1-55153-983-7	Alberta Titans	Susan Warrender
1-55153-982-9	Dinosaur Hunters	Lisa Murphy-Lamb
1-55153-970-5	Early Voyageurs	Marie Savage
1-55153-968-3	Edwin Alonzo Boyd	Nate Hendley
1-55153-996-9	Emily Carr	Cat Klerks
1-55153-992-6	Ghost Town Stories from the Red Coat Trail	Johnnie Bachusky
1-55153-993-4	Ghost Town Stories from the Canadian Rockies	Johnnie Bachusky
1-55153-969-1	Klondike Joe Boyle	Stan Sauerwein
1-55153-979-9	Ma Murray	Stan Sauerwein
1-55153-999-3	Mary Schäffer	Jill Foran
1-55153-962-4	Niagara Daredevils	Cheryl MacDonald
1-55153-981-0	Rattenbury	Stan Sauerwein
1-55153-991-8	Rebel Women	Linda Kupecek
1-55153-995-0	Rescue Dogs	Dale Portman
1-55153-998-5	Romance in the Rockies	Kim Mayberry
1-55153-997-7	Sam Steele	Holly Quan
1-55153-985-3	Tales from the Backcountry	Dale Portman
1-55153-986-1	Tales from the West Coast	Adrienne Mason
1-55153-994-2	The Heart of a Horse	Gayle Bunney
1-55153-989-6	Vancouver's Old-Time Scoundrels	Jill Foran
1-55153-987-X	Wilderness Tales	Peter Christensen
1-55153-980-2	Women Explorers	Helen Rolfe

These titles are available wherever you buy books. If you have trouble finding the book you want, call the Altitude order desk at 1-800-957-6888, e-mail your request to: orderdesk@altitudepublishing.com or visit our Web site at www.amazingstories.ca

All titles retail for $9.95 Cdn or $7.95 US. (Prices subject to change.)

New AMAZING STORIES titles are published every month. If you would like more information, e-mail your name and mailing address to: amazingstories@altitudepublishing.com.